FH INANLOU

How To Homeschool While Working

A Short Guide To Homeschool For The Working Parent

HOMESCHOOL WHILE WORKING

First edition

This book was professionally typeset on Reedsy.
Find out more at reedsy.com

Contents

Introduction

Look, I know what you're going through. You want the best for your child, but the traditional paths aren't working.

Some of you are done with public schools.

Some of you are done with private schools.

Some of you are planning for the future.

And some of you are simply looking for flexibility.

When homeschooling became an option, my knee-jerk reaction was, "That sounds overwhelming!" The idea of taking control of my child's education, let alone doing it while working, felt incredibly daunting. Homeschooling is only an option for the stay-at-home parent, right? How much will I have to give up?

- Do I need to quit my job?
- How much time can I really commit to teaching my children?
- Do I even know how to teach them well?
- I'm not familiar with Common Core, so how do I even begin, and how much time will that take to understand?

And what are the impacts to my child?

- Will she lose out on socializing?
- Will she test well and can compete with everyone else?

1

- How will college view a student who applies with a homeschooled transcript?

This book is not meant to teach you how to raise your child. It will not go over the different learning methods or the philosophy of what school should be about. This short book aims to demonstrate how obtainable it is to provide your children with a parent-designed education while maintaining a commitment to your career. By leveraging your existing skills, planning, and coordinating thoughtfully, you'll be set to homeschool while continuing to work.

1

Why Homeschool?

Since the era of the COVID-19 pandemic, when the world shut down and parents had no other choice but to repurpose their homes into mini learning centers, the conversation on homeschooling has grown. People have begun to see the value of parent-directed education, highlighting long-standing statistics.

According to the National Home Education Research Institute, children with home-based education score higher in standardized achievement tests (in the 15 to 25 percentile). They also attend college regularly, more regularly engage in social gatherings that support mental well-being, participate more often in civic engagement, and grow up to succeed.

Perhaps there isn't a need to convince you with statistics on the benefits of homeschooling. It's likely your conclusions are based on your observations that there is a growing opinion that the education system for both public and private schools has changed, and not for the better. I'm still tallying the number of times parents have reached out to me expressing their concerns about what their children are learning or *not* learning in school. Parents feel their values are being replaced with principles they don't agree with or consent to, and fear that a reduced quality of education that caters to the lowest performer leads to frustration and boredom for those who are ready for more.

I learned from an article by the Reason Foundation that 5.4% of American families with school-aged children surveyed in the 2024 U.S. Census Household Pulse Survey reported homeschooling their kids. That's almost double the pre-pandemic years (before 2020) when it was estimated only 2.8% of children were taught at home. Of the many reasons, families cited "concern for school environment" and "dissatisfaction with the academic instruction at other schools" as the top two reasons for their decision to homeschool.

Examples of Famous People Who Were Homeschooled

Here are a few notable figures from history and today who demonstrate the potential of homeschooled children:

- Thomas Edison, world-renown inventor
- Florence Nightingale, the founder of modern nursing
- Joseph Pulitzer, world-renowned newspaper editor
- Serena Williams, decorated Wimbledon tennis player
- Tim Tebow - NFL football player
- Emma Watson - child actor for the Harry Potter movie series
- Shaun White - world-renowned snowboarder

And while those above are well-known in history, sports, and entertainment, you'll find plenty of success stories in the business world, too. For Richard Lorenzen, homeschool education led him to found a multi-million-dollar business, Fifth Avenue Brands. The mother of a multimillionaire, Nathan Barry, credited his homeschool education to seeding his entrepreneurial spirit that built the marketing platform ConvertKit.

All these success stories share one common denominator: parents who trusted and invested in a framework centered around their child's interests. Some parents, like Shaun White's, held full-time jobs while coordinating a schedule that accommodated homeschooling and supported Shaun's travels around the world to become one of the greatest snowboarding athletes in history. I hope these success stories involving working parents will inspire you to see the possibilities in your own family.

Stories Of Working Parents Who Homeschool

Reducing the altitude, here are some observations of the people I know who are "super parents" in their own right. All names have been replaced for anonymity, of course.

1. Bakery Owner. Lisa was a former admissions counselor who now runs a successful pastry shop. While homeschooling her two children, she applied knowledge from her past career to create a pathway that allowed her daughter to pursue theater while finishing high school and completing college coursework. Her daughter helped out at the bakery, too! She is now enrolled at the University of California, Berkeley, and continues to perform in leading roles on stage.
2. Vaccine Scientist. Paul is a vaccine scientist running a team on the East Coast of the United States while working remotely from the West Coast. With this setup, Paul's work schedule starts at 5 am PST with a break for breakfast with his middle-school son. During his workday, his son is assigned coursework from personal

tutors sourced from local universities who provide customized, in-person lessons. Paul ends his work day by 2 pm and takes his son to on-site enrichment classes, such as martial arts, piano, and wildlife lessons in the afternoon.

3. Community Leader - Sandra spends most of her time on unpaid, voluntary work contributing to community development initiatives, including serving as a community center board member, organizing fundraisers, and coordinating cultural events. All this while raising five children. Even with her full plate, Sandra orchestrates an amazing schedule for all her children through in-person tutoring, online classes, and homeschool pods. Her eldest son recently graduated high school and is taking a gap year to invest in his business idea before beginning his PhD journey at California State University.

For many parents, these examples seem attainable to only a few with parent superpowers. I'm here to dispel that myth; homeschooling while working does not require superpowers. Homeschooling while working is obtainable when intentionally planned.

2

How To Start

The first step to homeschooling is having an interest in and a commitment to the idea of homeschooling your children, which has brought you here to this book. The next step is orienting yourself with the legalities of homeschooling based on where you live. As a disclaimer, this chapter is not meant to provide legal advice and I recommend consulting with your state institutions and legal services on the best options for you.

How Is Homeschool Defined?

"Homeschooling" is a rather loosely defined term. Some consider homeschooling as a purely home-based education and others consider it as learning outside of traditional public or private schools, where families have complete agency on what and how education is delivered. There are several models for homeschooling, and most fit into one of five categories:

1. **Traditional homeschooling** is where parents are responsible for deciding and delivering educational material.

2. *Unschooling* is where children pursue their interests and learn through self-directed activities rather than a structured curriculum.

3. *The Charlotte Mason Method* focuses on 'living books,' nature study, and short lessons to provide a broad and engaging education.

4. *The Montessori Method* emphasizes self-directed learning, hands-on activities, and mixed-age classrooms.

5. *Online homeschooling*, where online platforms are the primary form of the child's education.

Interestingly, these terminologies are not considered official education modalities under most laws and regulations. Some states don't even recognize the term 'homeschool' and will only identify the style as public or private school education. Depending on where you live, your options on how you homeschool will vary. Most states in the U.S. will expect you to file a notice of intent to homeschool and keep records of attendance. I recommend connecting with legal experts such as the Homeschool Legal Defense Association (https://hslda.org/), who not only offer legal advice but post wonderful material on their website relevant to the states and countries you plan to homeschool and work in.

For example, in California, "homeschool" is not legally recognized as an acceptable education modality. California parents will need to enroll their children in public school or under a private school affidavit, after which they can "homeschool" their children in three ways:

1. As a private school.
2. Through a private school satellite program.
3. Through a private tutor.

Another important point to be aware of is that parents who enroll their kids in a public charter school that offers them the option to select a curriculum may consider themselves "homeschooled". But legally, they are still participating in public school. While funded by the state, these public charter schools still have more independence than traditional schools and can choose to transfer some of that independence to the parents. For example, Visions in Education Charter School in Northern California will grant parents agency to select an approved curriculum and utilize a stipend to purchase materials and enrichment classes. However, this requires an approval process and the expectation is for students to submit work products regularly that meet state requirements. Again, while this structure uses public funds, I consider this model homeschool as, to a large degree, it gives parents autonomy on how and when their children's education is delivered.

Submit Your Intentions To Homeschool

If you live in a state or country where laws are favorable to homeschooling, you first need to understand the requirements for declaring your decision to homeschool. In California, you will need to file a Private School Affidavit (PSA) with the state, and prior, if your child is in an existing school, notify them of your exit plans. After giving notice, you can pursue your homeschool agenda, provided you meet the state requirements under the PSA.

In Massachusetts, where homeschooling is more strictly regulated, you must obtain approval before you homeschool. The school committee may review specific attributes of your application, including your competency to teach, the curriculum the child will follow, and the assessments being used.

3

Getting Ready

Change is a taxing adjustment for anyone at any age. And not every child can easily transition from a public or private school setting to homeschooling. This change means your child will now look up to you as their primary instructor. This chapter will delve into the crucial aspects of when to switch to homeschooling, how to recognize your child's learning style, and how to ensure they develop essential skills, including good manners, early reading habits, and the appropriate use of technology. We'll also inventory the skills and qualities *you* already possess to make this work.

When To Switch To Homeschool

Similar to common guidance on when to wean your baby off of their pacifier, the best time to get your child used to homeschooling is early. According to some, there is a "safe range" for switching a child to homeschool or returning to public or private school without significantly impacting their learning journey. The table below provides general guidance I've put together based on my observations and discussions with experienced homeschool parents.

SUGGESTED GRADE LEVEL TO SWITCH TO HOMESCHOOL

Switch OK✓	Caution ✗
Kindergarten to Grade 2	Grade 3
Grade 4 to 6	Grade 7 to 8
Grade 9 to 12	

The table above groups ages in buckets and considers when children are likely going through a significant developmental phase. For example, in Grade 3, students are typically in the beginning stages of mastering certain math concepts, so switching at this time may lead to confusion or setbacks. Beast Academy, a mastery curriculum with its particular teaching style, offers its curriculum between Grades 3 and 5. I rarely recommend that students move in or out of homeschool if they cannot maintain the same math pedagogy, especially if it's proving effective. Equally, children between 7th and 8th grade are likely in a period where strong connections and relationships are being established. If you start homeschooling in a middle school grade, ensure your children continue to have access to the healthy social connections they established. Otherwise, it is best avoided as emotional consequences may greatly hinder the benefits homeschooling was meant to offer.

I recommend switching to homeschooling before Grade 3 or waiting until your child enters 6th Grade. Once in middle school, many parents observe rapid changes in their child's physical, emotional, and social qualities. Academically, they are transitioning from an elementary school environment that is more controlling to a setting that demands greater independence and responsibility. And at the same time, they may grapple with identity formation and self-esteem issues, as they seek to establish their place within their peer groups. At this time, it's crucial to have your child be part of the decision-making process regarding schedules and what they want to focus on. Also, ensure there are opportunities for social interactions, emotional support, and activities that foster both academic and personal growth.

Determine Your Child's Learning Style

According to Ability Path there are four main ways of learning:

1. *Visual:* learn through seeing
2. *Auditory:* learn through hearing
3. *Tactile:* learn through touch
4. *Kinesthetic:* learn through doing and moving)

Kids grasp knowledge in one of these ways and recognize which can greatly improve their learning experience. Adapting to your child's preferred learning style can personalize your homeschooling approach, making the learning process more effective and enjoyable. Here's a quick summary of how to tell which learning style your child may favor:

Visual Learners

Visual learners absorb information through what they see. You tend to see more interest when they are reading or observing demonstrations or using visual aids such as videos, charts, and diagrams. My daughter is a visual learner, and at first, I thought she ignored me when she doodled while I presented new ideas. It later occurred to me that her doodling helped her process information because of her ability to reflect deeply on key topics.

Auditory Learners

Auditory learners love to listen to discussions and stories. They tend to have really good memory but are easily distracted by background noise. Because of this, it's especially important to ensure the learning space is quiet and instructions are repeated verbally.

Tactile Learners

Hands-on learners are seen as "tactile" and love to fidget with objects and materials to experience learning. Like visual learners, you'll see them draw, but they will also look for objects and representations as references to fully understand a concept. You can find tactile adults in the office fidgeting with the company desk toys as they participate in conference calls. You may even be one of them!

Kinesthetic

Playfully referred to as "dancing learners", kinesthetic children prefer movement and physical activity. When a kinesthetic learner is confined to a seated position, you will notice their feet tapping or them often getting out of their chair. When I see this, I opt to teach a lesson outside for subjects like physics, math, and science. Using theater or improv tends to be the most effective for history or literature.

Your child will lean towards multiple learning styles, but there is no hard and fast rule that these attributes don't overlap. For example, I know my daughter learns best through auditory and visual cues. So, to maximize her learning experience, I'll select a curriculum that includes easy-to-visualize exercises or supplemental videos. When assessing an instructor or tutor, I look for someone who can emphasize concepts through fun stories.

By recognizing and adapting to your child's learning style, you can create a tailored and successful homeschooling experience that supports their academic development and instills a lifelong passion for gaining knowledge.

Manners

The best feeling is when someone comes up to me complimenting my children's manners; and how considerate and thoughtful they are. Ultimately, children will decide how they present themself to the world. Still, in the impressionable stages, it is very important for us, as parents and guardians, to set the expectations of how to engage and when to activate certain behaviors. This creates mutual respect between a child and a parent, especially regarding instructions. It's the job of parents to demonstrate to their children that good manners are expected in public settings and family gatherings and how to be in a shared space as you work and they navigate their school day around you.

As you introduce a homeschool rhythm, your child will understand that learning is a gift and that the best moments are spent with curiosity and excitement while being respectful.

Encourage Reading Early

When juggling responsibilities, which include homeschooling and your work, it is crucial that your homeschooled child becomes self-sufficient in their learning responsibilities. When children learn how to read early, it not only gives them an advantage, but it also helps their parents. As we prepared for our second daughter to enter homeschool, I immediately prioritized 15 minutes each day to go through the Learning Dynamics series with her (available at https://4weekstoread.com/). Before summer ended, our 5-year-old developed the confidence to read basic sentences. From kindergarten onward, she began every parent-led assignment by pointing and reading the instructions with me.

Encourage Appropriate Use Of Technology Early

In the current world we live in, digital literacy is imperative. This excludes screen time for entertainment, video gaming, and social media. In this context, it's about a child's familiarity with joining online meetings, understanding the concept of file structures, and how to type and view calendars. With proper instruction and practice, children can log into their computer and join an online class as early as kindergarten, relieving you from the technology setup. You can invite your child to sit close to you for the online class while you continue your work.

I must add that while my children can access technology, I do have rules to ensure they focus on the task assigned. At my house, we set parental controls using features on our smartphones to ensure only appropriate applications and content are available.

In summary, start early and consider the best times to transition to homeschooling, typically before 3rd Grade or after 6th Grade. Remember that understanding and responding to your child's learning style—whether visual, auditory, tactile, or kinesthetic—can significantly enhance their educational experience. Finally, good manners should be instilled by encouraging early reading and digital literacy. These skills foster independence, respect, and the ability to navigate technology, which is essential for modern learning environments.

Getting Yourself Ready

You know you already have the skills to create a beautiful and productive homeschool journey. As a parent in a digitally dominated world, you are likely juggling work and family responsibilities and are comfortable using technology; you are familiar with using online calendars, have a reasonable comfort level in researching topics, and are prepared to allocate the budget needed for your child's learning experiences. Let's discuss more on what this means.

Get Computer Literate

These days, it's expected that you possess basic computer literacy, and in many places, knowing how to use a smartphone is common knowledge. Whether you enroll your homeschooled child online or in person, using computers to register, track, and complete class and work assignments is common practice. As a homeschool parent, prepare to be your child's tech support and be ready to learn something new always. I started with basic knowledge of how to connect to the internet, computers, and printing machines. Through the years, I learned to troubleshoot across different operating systems and new gadgets, which enhanced my child's virtual classroom experience.

Get Familiar With Using Online Calendars

While this sounds basic, learning to use a calendar effectively is key to juggling your day with a homeschooled child, even if you are not working.

My world does not function without the help of an online calendar. Here, l use colorful tiles organized by work, homeschool, and family time. It helps me quickly size up my day and prompts me to adjust, especially when family time does not appear during the week. I like to track activities day by day and subject-by-subject. Take advantage of labeling, color coding, and features that allow you to share with those who benefit from it. My calendar is shared with caregivers, tutors, grandparents, and even those marked as emergency contacts for my children.

Get Comfortable With Researching Topics

As a homeschool parent, you are automatically a research scientist, constantly searching for your child's best curriculum or class. You will also learn or re-learn concepts in preparation for that deep-dive discussion for a particular assignment. I didn't expect my daughter to be interested in chemistry in the 5th Grade and found myself reviewing The Periodic Table in case she came to me with additional questions.

If you are a working parent, you may not have time to spend on research. So, consider homeschool support services, whether paid or free, to answer your questions. If you don't have time to review The Periodic Table, connect your child to a tutor. If you don't have time to search for the best curriculum, find experts who can offer options and advice tailored to your situation.

Sometimes, answers to questions will come from your networks. Homeschool parents are always happy to share, and the power of community, word of mouth, and advice always yield valuable information.

Reserve Budget Towards Child's Learning

Generally, families who homeschool with minimal cost will have an adult fully committed to delivering the education. However, as a working parent, your options expand when you spend dollars on your child's learning.

My recommendation to working parents is to commit to a budget of some sort. Especially during the elementary and middle school years, more likely than not, you won't have the capacity to teach every subject. In our house, we re-purposed a portion of our budget originally planned for private school towards in-person, subject-focused classes. We also help pay for gas to parents who agree to drive and drop off our kids at their activities, and, for a while, we hired a caregiver to help us with our children's schedules.

Check out the section "How Much Will This Cost Me?" for more information.

4

Creating Your Homeschool Environment

How you set up your environment will directly impact how you experience homeschooling. Given that your home will now be purposed for rest, work, and learning, it is ever more important to be intentional about what is placed and where.

If you are already someone who works from home or has reserved a place to work at home, your area is likely equipped with an ergonomic chair, a reliable computer, and necessary office supplies to boost focus and productivity. Similarly, when preparing a learning area for your child, you should consider physical, visual, and ambiance elements that enable her to focus. We'll go over eight considerations:

1. Dedicated space for learning and working
2. Implement a family policy on technology
3. Create a visible schedule
4. Remove distractions
5. Dedicate a space for breaks
6. Make seasonal changes visible and celebrate work
7. Have appropriate supplies

8. Create daily ceremonies

1. Dedicated Space For Learning and Working

The benefits of a student being homeschooled can also be a disadvantage. While we boast how wonderful it is to learn in the comfort of your own home, it may easily be a space for non-productivity, anxiety, and frustration. Children can easily be confused about how to enter a space without clear definitions of how and when a space is used for learning.

Whether your space is a studio apartment or whether you have a separate accessory dwelling unit (ADU), make sure there are conversations about the expectations in each part of the house when the homeschool schedule is activated. For younger ones, you can send this message indirectly by consistently choosing a space to read together. Ensure the area is free from things that will distract learners and stocked with supplies and visuals that prompt an academic mindset.

With space comes sound. As you define your work, school, and leisure areas, set the expectation that your child lowers her voice and calms down as she approaches or passes your area. In return, when you enter her space, you refrain from noisy multi-tasking and avoid doing things that prevent you from giving her your full attention. Mutual respect for boundaries and a clear understanding of how to posture oneself in these will create a conducive space for learning.

2. Implement A Family Policy On Technology

Regarding homeschooling and technology, people conjure up an image of a teenager sitting in bed surfing the internet. At the same time, another screen remains open, and her online class runs on autopilot and is ignored. Many homeschooled children will frequently find themselves with spare time either because of a large gap between activities or because they completed an assignment early. Without a family policy on technology, children may resort to entertaining themselves with a screen, gaming, or the like.

I highly recommend designating a space where technology, including laptops and tablets, is used and stored. Having a "tech check-in/checkout" system will convey the message that technology is a utility primarily used for learning and not entertainment, especially in the times allocated for school work. In our house, we require all tech interactions, including smartphones, to occur in a public space such as the living room or next to a parent. If sharing physical space while using technology is impossible, I recommend installing parental control software that limits what applications and features can be used.

The following illustration visually summarizes our home philosophy about technology: Technology is only allowed in shared spaces such as the living room, kitchen, and office. While work can be done in the bedrooms, anything requiring technology is not allowed, including laptops used for homework assignments.

HOME POLICY FOR TECH

KITCHEN

LIVING ROOM

BATHROOM

OFFICE

BEDROOM

BEDROOM

3. Create A Visible Schedule

Creating boundaries as they relate to time is so important. While your online calendars actively hold information on activities planned for the day, transferring it into a visible schedule board or hanging calendar re-emphasizes the message of structure that is to be followed (and occasionally negotiated.) It can also help you facilitate a daily morning ceremony to review the day's activities. This can take a few minutes and is most effective for younger children to do daily, where they can check off their assigned tasks. You can adjust the frequency to weekly or longer as they age.

SCHEDULE BOARD

have child engage and keep track of tasks

track completion

simple chalkboard

updated daily

4. Remove Distractions

There are many beautiful ways in which parents organize their work area and supply space, but the key is to ensure they remain organized.

Allowing materials to pile up can distract you and your child. For example, when the science equipment is still sitting on the table that your child is using to write her English paper, it inadvertently becomes a distraction, and she will spend more time touching it than completing the work at hand.

Auditory learners can be sensitive to sound. Find ways to address the ambiance if the space is near a buzzing vent, loud clock, active dishwasher (or worse), near you and your audible conference calls. Invest in noise-canceling headphones to allow her to concentrate regardless of the audible commotion in her environment. Noise-canceling headphones are handy, especially when the space carries sound, and you are in an online meeting.

Finally, storage options such as shelves, bins, and organizers should be utilized to maintain tidiness and ensure children can easily access these items when needed.

5. Dedicate A Space for Breaks

Allocating time and space to take breaks is one of the best things about homeschooling while working. Unlike other parents, you are accessible to your children most of the day and have the opportunity to build moments that matter with them more frequently. Storytime can happen in your 15-minute break, and breakfast and lunch will feel less rushed with just a few steps into the kitchen.

As kids get older, they will want to use breaks on their own terms. I recommend they not access social media. Break time used for mindless scrolling can impact mental health, which continues to be worrisome, as expressed in an article by Health Day titled, "1 in 5 U.S. Parents Worry

Their Teen Is Addicted to the Internet". Despite the short break, it can be difficult for children to switch back to focus on work. To counter, consider adding an "options board" that lists alternative activities your child can choose while waiting for their next assigned work. In our house, this list is pinned next to the schedule wall and laminated, where our daughters can use a dry-erase marker to check off the activity of choice. For younger children, this gives them a sense of agency and self-governance while you have a sense of assurance they are occupied with more beneficial activities.

Example list of options to choose from while on breaks or in between scheduled assignments:

- Read a chapter book
- Play a board game
- Practice typing
- Help the adult in your family with house chores
- Practice spelling
- Journal
- Draw, do arts & crafts
- Memorize state capital
- Practice tying your shoes
- Knit
- Clean your room
- Learn how to roller-skate
- Go through math drills
- Play basketball
- Do core exercises (50 sit-ups, 20 push-ups, 20 burpees)

6. Make Seasonal Changes Visible And Celebrate Work

Decorating the learning environment to acknowledge seasonal changes and key celebrations can really lift the mood of your home and reinforce the message that your home is a learning space. Limit the decor to a certain area in the house where you can prompt conversation about a specific topic. Consistent with my comments on distractions, try to avoid places where focused study occurs and set it up in places where breaks occur or even in the hallway on your way out the door. In my house, we leverage the bay window in the living room to display seasonal changes.

SEASONAL CHANGES

Dedicate a Corner

Persian New Year to welcome Spring.

Fall leaves to prepare for Autumn.

BRAG BOARD

consider changing content
after each learning period

writing assignment

show case art

simple glass frame hung
in a visible place to
acknowledge good work.

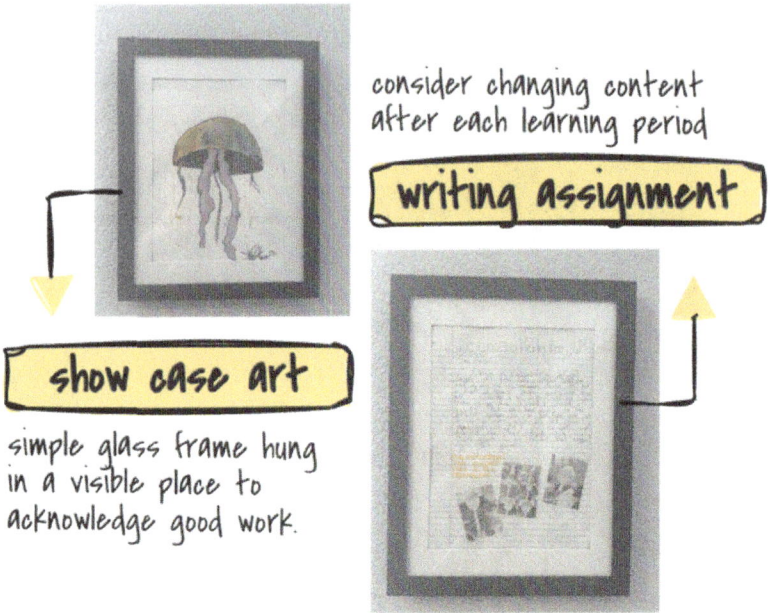

7. Have Appropriate Supplies

Manipulative, Representation, and Supplemental Tools

While technology's progress has enabled virtual learning, I believe concepts are best understood in the physical—or, as the saying goes, "IRL—in real life." For kinesthetic learners, touching objects and getting hands-on experience offers so much more than what virtual reality can truly achieve. Even for auditory and visual learners, the senses received from acoustics and live presence go beyond what 3D and surround sound can give.

With that, I recommend complementing your curriculum with manipulative representations and supplemental tools that are age-appropriate and relevant to the subject. I arrange supplemental into three categories:

1. Manipulative typically refers to STEM subjects (Science, Technology, Engineering, and Mathematics) that include blocks, measuring kits, number lines, counters, scales, and patterns.
2. Representations. Examples include globes, chemistry models, and circuit kits encouraging analytical thinking.
3. Other supplemental tools. These include a magnifying glass, coloring tools, tracing paper, and dry-erase boards. I will also include speech and social development material, such as sequencing cards, to help students bring key ideas home.

Some vendors will package manipulatives and representations with their curricula so parents do not have to take the extra step of procuring them. However, I recommend you review them to ascertain whether they will be effective for your child in the context of his or her learning style and adjust.

MANIPULATIVE

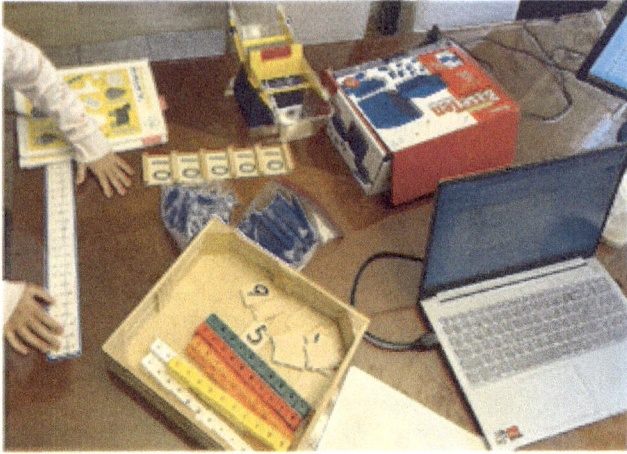

Ensure manipulative matches learning style

Supplies and Equipment

For online classes and working with online tutors, set up the desk with equipment that enhances the video experience. What I find worth investing in are tablet holders, headsets with microphones, and lighting. When my homeschooler joins a class with an online personal tutor, we have her join from two video angles:

(1) Face recording, and

(2) One that directly hovers over her writing desk.

This lets the instructor see the work and create an in-person experience. Of course, if the online class only involves online work, sharing a desktop through the conference call app will suffice.

SET UP FOR ONLINE CLASS

clamps to table
& adjustable

tablet holder

tablet
log in with camera
pointing at deskwork

2nd camera
smart phone, tablet or
laptop log in with
camera facing child

Continuing the list of supplies, including a mini library and basic office supplies, including a printer, markers, and label makers. For younger students, include stickers or stamps to use for completed works. Ensure supplies are stocked and arranged as intended. Organize the supplies by categories that facilitate easy discovery and put the most frequently used supplies in the most accessible storage part.

8. Create Daily Ceremonies

Birthdays, holidays, seasons, and end-of-school-year parties. We are a creature of traditions where celebrations move something within us - whether it be acknowledging an accomplishment or orienting us with the changes happening to us. This is no different when approaching a homeschool rhythm (which we'll get to in more detail later in this book).

Ceremonies to signify the start and end of formal learning are key, especially for elementary school children. I underestimated the importance of recess, line-ups, and the morning principal message until I became a mother to homeschooled children. When the physical space is used for both home and school, transitioning your mindset can be difficult for anyone at any age!

In my house, we start the day with mindfulness exercises and gratitude. The five minutes of quiet help us decouple from what was before and focus on the day ahead. I then walk over to our wooden-framed agenda board that hangs between our living room wall to go over the planned day. This was repeated daily until the fifth grade when it became weekly.

For the beginning and end of the school year, I like to incorporate bridging ceremonies that reserve time for parents and extended family supporters to reflect on the road traveled and the road ahead. Whether small or large, the key is to separate it from the usual. This can be done over a special meal, ceremonial walks across a physical bridge, stairs, or pathway, or any ritual you believe will set that moment apart. At our house, bridging ceremonies have varied from a 15-minute walk down the hallway with a flowered crown at the end to a tea party with their friends. If you plan to teach year-round, consider other major milestones, such as the end of the project or capstones.

Implementing ceremonies to usher routines, however mundane or important, not only gives the child something to look forward to, it demonstrates the attention you as a parent are giving to their learning journey. Additionally, ceremonies and routines give the children structure and promote self-governance.

Invite Feedback: The Parent-Child Journal

Journaling has always been a key part of my life due to its many benefits. It allows me to reflect, correct, and plan how I approach the world and my optics about it. It is like a feedback loop to yourself. This technique can also be applied with your homeschooled child as another layer of honest communication and commitment to responding to and resolving issues that surface in that exchange.

Journaling with my children began when I sensed compression between us through our intertwined work meetings, in-person classes, and extracurricular activities. As soon as they knew how to draw and write basic sentences, I introduced the idea of a "mommy-daughter journal." For each child, I gifted a single leather-bound lined journal stamped with an elephant that would get pulled in the evenings of those hard days. They would start with a page and write or draw how they felt that day. In return, I will give my response on the following page. When they were younger, there were many pictures, hearts and simple words of "great job", "I love you" and "I'm sorry". As years passed, the pages became more sophisticated with thoughts and suggestions.

Being an effective homeschooling family works when both parent and child feel heard and understood. Constant feedback through journaling, I find, is an excellent way to fortify your commitment to each other during this special journey.

The School Year Binder

The school year binder has a particular significance for the homeschool parent. Not only is it used to capture the child's work product, but it can also be used as a time capsule to track learning progress and prompt conversations to reflect back on the school year that has passed. Right before summer starts, I will gather the children to review their work with me. It's fantastic to see their eyes light up as they observe how much they've changed within a span of 8 to 10 months, noting the evolution of their handwriting and thinking.

The binder can be created and maintained from the first day of school. It can include written work, pictures of projects, learning moments, and achievement certificates. Through the years, you will build a library of binders reflecting all the beautiful moments spent together learning.

OUR BINDER!

Binder structure

- print out all work
- include selected online items
- add any certificates earned
- add pictures taken
- separated by learning period & subject

A proper homeschool environment involves preparing our family and physical environment and implementing family policies that support learning in the home. I wouldn't be surprised if you already implemented a version of one or more of the items listed in this chapter. Look around; you may already be ready to both homeschool and work!

5

Curriculum Mapping: What Is It?

Curriculum mapping plays a key role in your planning by aligning teaching methods with learning objectives, standards, and specific educational aims. It reflects your personal approach to keeping your child on track with their learning growth goals. The process can get quite involved, but it's not something you have to do alone. You can follow curriculum already created by other homeschool parents and adjust as needed or leverage services like www.homeschoolandworking.com, which will assist you in building your own curriculum. See the section on Delegating to learn more.

There are many ways to develop a curriculum map, and, in general, they fit into these seven steps:

Step 1: Select A Learning Standard

For families who plan to take state assessments, select a learning standard to build their curriculum map. The United States uses the Common Core State Standards, but you should also look into your state or country to understand what is expected from general education.

Step 2: Evaluate Your Child's Abilities

Evaluate your child's abilities, identify their strengths, and note areas for improvement. You can use tests from records, utilize online assessments, or get proctored by a certified test provider. Choosing what fits you will likely depend on the requirements established in your state or country. It's meant to help you tailor the curriculum to meet your child's needs.

There are many differing opinions on the value of assessments, their impact, and reservations about the idea in its entirety. However, I see benefits, and incorporating the practice of assessments into your curriculum will create familiarity and strengthen a muscle required if they choose to enroll in universities or obtain certifications that require testing.

Step 3: Develop Measurable Objectives

Develop measurable learning objectives for each subject based on standards and assessments. For instance, in mathematics, a goal could be, "By the end of the year, my child will be proficient in solving step word problems involving fractions." This goal will be aligned to a particular standard in mathematics for the particular grade level. You can also measure the objective by an "I Can" statement that describes the learning target and outcomes in a way a child will understand. You can find "I Can" statements online for the Common Core State Standards.

Step 4: Choose Curriculum Materials

Next, choose curriculum materials that align with your child's learning objectives. You can take this onboard in many ways. The easiest is to follow along with an existing homeschool family you trust or obtain recommendations from homeschool consultants and credentialed teachers. If part of your plan is to enroll in a learning pod that is subject-focused, the curriculum is likely selected for you.

The most involved and most tailored way to choose a curriculum is to research and identify available resources from scratch. One way to start is to attend a curriculum fair in your area. Here, you will have the opportunity to speak directly with vendors and get your questions answered.

Certain curricula can span several grades, intersect subjects, or both. Moving Beyond the Page, for example, is a comprehensive curriculum covering science, language arts, and history. One package can be taught through three school grades, including all the storybooks and science materials.

A tip I'd like to share when selecting a curriculum is to make sure you analyze the teacher's manual and review the table of contents and teaching method to give you a sense of what is involved. You may want to acquire additional manipulatives to enhance the assignment, making it more effective for your child. You should also determine if some or all of the curriculum is what you want to delegate or teach directly.

Step 5: Integrate Subjects Where Possible

Consider blending subjects to offer a well-rounded learning experience. For instance, a science project could involve math, reading, and writing. You can weave the learning topic throughout the day to reinforce key concepts. For example, our Girl Scout troop focused on the water cycle, which aligned with part of my science curriculum for my 3rd grader. Given my original plan was to go over it in the spring while the Girl Scouts introduced it in the fall, I adjusted the timing and sequence to match the Girl Scout outings. During Asian Pacific Islander Heritage Month, I also included foods from different parts of the region in our snack break. When we visited Italy with family, we stopped in Pompeii to witness the remnants of ancient volcanic activity and mysterious history that aligned with my 5th grader's literature assignment. The intentional weaving of concepts demonstrates that learning is a continuous process and is engaging and fun!

Step 6: Pace Curriculum

Now that you have a map that threads your learning standards, assessments, and curriculum material, pace out how topics will be deployed. The idea here is to outline how and when different topics and subjects will be taught throughout your defined school year or learning period. It involves setting a timeline to ensure all learning activities are in a logical and manageable sequence that works for both you and your child.

If you plan to enroll your child in learning, this pace will already be laid out. But for those subjects you are in complete control of with pacing, start by looking at the entire curriculum as a pie and divide the goals into individual slices or modules. I recommend not to plan any less than a week and no less than a month. This will allow you to respond to unexpected changes while still accomplishing your learning goals. For monthly planning, you can set aside which parts of the month are designated for concentrated work and which parts are more relaxed to accommodate your work priorities. See more details in my chapter on Time Management.

Step 7: Constantly Reassess

Reserve times throughout the year to re-assess if the learning materials are effective for your child and meet the required standards. This can be done through short quizzes, but many of us can quickly identify it through observation. While nothing stops you from adjusting your child's curriculum plan, I recommend you commit to the learning objectives specifically related to the core subjects. If you find you need more time, then extend the learning. If you find the content insufficient or ineffective, look for other learning materials. This is the best part about homeschooling because you can identify gaps and strengths more frequently.

With the right planning, you can create a comprehensive, engaging, and memorable learning experience for your children. I've attached a curriculum map example at the end of this book.

CURRICULUM MAP

Planning each learning period for the month allows for flexibility while maintaining accountability to the learning objective.

STUDENT NAME
GRADE

CURRICULUM	MONTH 1	MONTH 2	MONTH 3

This is usually the vendor name or title of material or class name

Curriculum Name

Final deliverable name or assignment name & page in the curriculum material

More assignments and work product to commit to from the curriculum.

More assignments and work product to commit to from the curriculum.

I like to only name the final deliverable. This gives me flexibility in case we can skip or dive deeper on specific assignments

Diagnostics

Assess how things are going. This can also include feedback loop with your child and identify what works.

STANDARDS

For each learning period, indicate the learning objective or standard it aligns with. Ensure all your objectives are mapped by end of school year.

OPPORTUNITIES

Use Of Artificial Intelligence

Nowadays, it's hard to avoid discussing artificial intelligence (AI). And we certainly won't ignore it in this book. There is a huge opportunity in the homeschool world to use AI-based solutions, even more so for working parents who homeschool. With effective prompting, parents can use AI to assist with building their curriculum, automate planning, and compile resources tailored to their child's learning objectives. While there are commercial solutions to assisting educators with curriculum building using AI, I have yet to find, at the writing of this book, a great AI tool that caters to the homeschool family. The ones I've looked into claim to produce curriculum content or refer to existing curricula, but it's still just one part of the full picture of curriculum development.

For me, the curriculum is more than just absorbing content. It also maps learning objectives to in-person experiences, including classes, field trips, workshops, and events. There will be a day when AI solutions can inventory both formal vendors and informal community events posted on social media to propose a personalized curriculum that integrates both online and in-person learning.

Until then, I recommend we strengthen the new AI muscle of "prompting," which involves using specific words that effectively command the technology to return a desired result. Example prompts to use with curriculum building include:

```
"Design a comprehensive 10-week curriculum for a 7th-grade
student focusing on American History. Include key topics,
weekly goals, and suggested readings."

"Create a daily lesson plan for a high school biology course
that includes interactive activities, videos, and
assessments."

"Provide a list of online resources and books for teaching
calculus to high school students that meets Washington state
public school standards."
```

6

Types Of Classes And Learning Experiences

The availability of educational content has soared in the past decade, and it's exciting to see. No longer is a homeschooled child seen learning in isolation, but rather, they can access and immerse in a global community through various mediums, including online classes, private tutors, subject-specific pods, micro-schools, and co-ops. Let's go over the types of classes and learning experiences working parents are incorporating into their curriculum.

Parent Instructed Learning

Parent-instructed learning is the most common image of what home-schooling looks like. Here, parents take full responsibility and account-ability for designing their curriculum and teaching their children. I think this can work when your child is between kindergarten and 2nd Grade, as the time for core learning is generally between 60 to 90 minutes per day. This can definitely be inserted into your work schedule if you can align it with how your child learns best or spread it throughout the day. However, you will still need to incorporate care giving, which this age range requires more. As your child gets older, you will find they are more self-sufficient, and your participation in the teaching changes for the better. As a parent who works full-time, I prefer combining the curriculum with what I can teach and with experts I find to teach.

Remember, parent-instructed learning happens all the time and seamlessly. From making breakfast together to a car ride spent reflecting on current events, you can learn life skills and core subjects at any time. As a parent with a homeschooled child, you are always teaching.

Online Classes

Online classes are a boon for working parents, offering flexibility and a wealth of resources at your fingertips. These courses range from complete curricula to supplementary classes in specific subjects. Some known platforms such as Khan Academy, Time4Learning, and Connections Academy provide structured, full-year programs covering all core subjects. iXL.com and Synthesis also have adaptive learning features. These were quite popular during the "lockdown days" of COVID-19. Parents treated them as supplemental and even replacements on subjects poorly taught by schools attempting to transition from a seated to an online modality.

I look for online classes with the most personal and in-person experience possible. Platforms like Outschool offer recorded and group classes and one-on-one private classes where you can negotiate or help custom configure alongside the instructor. The online courses I prefer include materials that are sent to your house. This is especially helpful in bringing concepts like science, physics, and chemistry to life. Vendors like Generation Genius and Quantum Camp will mail the beakers, microscope, lenses, and solutions so you can follow along with their labs.

The diffusion that occurs when you are present with people is of obvious value, so I prefer to mix online and in-person classes.

Private Tutoring

If your child responds better with individualized attention, sourcing a private tutor is the way to go. The work involved here is finding the right person who fits your child's learning style, schedule, and budget. Similar to recruiting firms, there are national services that, for a fee, will connect you with one of their hired tutors.

I have been successful in finding tutors through referrals from my networks. My child's math tutor came from a science pod from a prior year, another parent referred our credentialed literature teacher, and many of the music teachers in the area offer excellent high school chemistry support. With private tutoring, you directly influence how the learning will be given to your child, and requests for adjustments are almost immediate.

In-Person Enrichment

Depending on your location, you may have access to a wealth of in-person enrichment classes. The owners of these establishments range from large vendors to individual proprietors. When selecting, my first preference is to evaluate the in-person enrichment classes near me to determine if they can be the main teaching source or supplement a subject.

My children respond well to math centers like the Art of Problem

Solving, which offers in-person classes once a week with homework (both online and workbook) to complete before the next class. Similarly, there are certified teachers who offer literature and history, like the Institute of Excellence in Writing (IEW). With IEW, the format is similar, with weekly classes, writing papers, and memorizing poetry.

In-person classes are especially necessary for nature-based learning. Also referred to as outdoor education, it has come a long way and is increasingly offered to primary education as early as pre-kindergarten. Today, especially with the negative impacts on mental wellness that technology screen time is causing, I see nature-based learning as an imperative to support physical health, mental well-being, and academic achievement. These classes can be offered as a full day or weekly. You can find outdoor classes in an existing establishment, like state parks, community recreational centers, or science centers. We found homeschool classes offered by a nearby wildlife rehabilitation center, which my daughter attended in person weekly and where she learned about freshwater habitats. Her classes ended with a ceremonial release of wild salmon at the end of the 10-week session. Know that nature-based learning is not limited to rural communities anymore. You can find them in urban settings like the Trackers Bay Area, which has a site in Berkeley, California.

Nature-Based Learning

Referred to as outdoor education, it has come a long way and is increasingly offered to primary education as early as pre-kindergarten. Today, especially with the negative impacts on mental wellness that technology screen time is causing, I see nature-based learning as imperative to support physical health, mental well-being, and academic achievement. Outdoor classes are offered through existing establishments such as state parks, community recreational centers, or science centers. These classes can be offered as a full day or weekly. We discovered the nearby wildlife rehabilitation center offered outdoor science labs, which my daughter attended in person and learned about freshwater habitats. We ended the 10-week session with a ceremonial release of wild salmon at the program's conclusion. Know that nature-based learning is not limited to rural communities anymore. You can find them in urban settings such as Trackers Bay Area, which has a site in Berkeley, California.

Co-Ops

The idea of a co-op suggests a community that shares the same values and collectively organizes a learning environment for their children for the entire school year. This means all families come together to purchase supplies and services and commit to teaching the curriculum. A co-op can take the form of a "formerly organized" or "casual" co-op.

Some co-ops require a time investment of as much as 15 to 20 hours per week, where parents are required to develop the curriculum, prepare labs, and tend to the property. For the parent who works full-time, this may be unduly straining unless the co-op is located close to home or meets in a schedule that aligns with your work responsibilities. While I've yet to find a co-op conducive to my schedule, it remains an option, given you can negotiate your parent's contribution to reasonable responsibilities without burning yourself out.

Micro Schools

Micro schools possess certain qualities similar to a co-op but transfer the teaching responsibilities to a hired qualified educator. Another attribute associated with micro schools is their use of educational technology, where learning is online, assignments are more hands-on, and in-person meetings are less frequent unless families agree to meet consistently at the teaching location. It is thought that about a million children in the United States are enrolled in a micro-school and growing. This can be a great option for working parents, but similar to a co-op, commitment is attached to a social contract with strict rules for canceling out because of the small group size of four to fifteen children.

Subject Focused Pods

If you can't commit to a co-op or micro-school for one year, I highly recommend connecting with parents to form subject-focused pods. This happens when parents come together and negotiate with an existing vendor or convince an educator to offer a course specific to their group of kids lasting for less than a school year. I use the term "subject-focused pods" as in-person or hybrid engagement, bringing together no more than 12 students regularly to learn about a specific subject for a few weeks at a time. While similar to in-person enrichment, it is usually supported by the coordination of parents and disbands after the course is completed. These pods are usually from spin-offs of previous classes where parents and students have connected before.

Amazing things can happen under the power of collective negotiation. Check out some examples I witnessed by reading stories in the Community section.

Sports

You can access sports through several sources, including community recreational centers, religious centers, commercial offerings, and even through public schools. Depending on your location, your high school may allow your child to participate in their sports program if you are enrolled in a public independent study program such as a charter homeschool funded by the state. Sports are worth considering as a class type for homeschooled children because, in addition to developing knowledge of the physical self, topics such as life skills, math, and science can also surface when you play a sport. For example, with my children in a soccer league this year, I will periodically require them to write a reflection paper on how their games connect with their current learning about physics, science, math, and social studies.

When selecting a class, evaluating whether it will be a main teaching source or supplement key ideas is important. Do this by reconciling the learning objectives you identified in your curriculum development with the syllabus or description.

In summary, there are many ways in which education is offered outside the traditional full-day seated models. It always surprises friends when I share how I configure our school year using all these class types. Most of these offerings organize the students across a grade or age range, allowing students to learn as deeply or widely as they find interest. The best part about participating in these class types is that you and your child have complete agency in selecting what works for you.

7

Time Management

Homeschooling sounds like a great idea, but where do you find the time? Time management is the undercurrent that determines whether you and your child feel homeschooling works. Even with committed intentions and the best curriculum selected, success does not happen unless you sequence and pace teaching in a manner that is effective and sustainable for you and your family. This section focuses on designing a sustainable pace and rhythm for you and your family.

Pacing

A pacing guide is a schedule that outlines what will be taught and when it will be covered. It'll help you ensure all necessary material is covered within a specific time frame and is an invaluable tool for homeschooling parents who work. By separating the curriculum into manageable units distributed throughout the teaching period and juxtaposing it with your work schedule, you will have a structured approach that fits your child's needs and your family's schedule.

To start, I recommend you take advantage of the examples that are already out there. The internet will offer you a plethora of ways to pace and sources like those posted on TeachersPayTeachers.com, which offers both free and paid versions. If you decide to enroll with a public charter homeschool, the credentialed teacher assigned to you will also offer a template. In general, a pacing guide will contain the following attributes:

1. The learning objective.
2. The curriculum.
3. The curriculum learning topic.
4. The learning period in which the curriculum learning topic will be introduced.

Depending on how finely detailed you wish to plan, pacing guidelines can be organized by quarters, months, and weeks. Below are some pro tips for building a practical pacing guide:

- Consider the average learning hours for each educational stage. Educational stages are usually divided into primary (elementary from kindergarten to Grade 5), secondary (middle school Grades 6 to 8), and tertiary (high school Grades 9 to 12). Students in elementary grades study for 15 to 20 hours per week, increasing in middle school to 20-25 hours. Students in high school can spend up to 30 hours learning per week.

- The curriculum learning topic is usually outlined in a table of contents in the teacher's manual of the curriculum material. For enrolled classes, they will be described in the syllabus. Reconcile this list with your learning objectives and confirm it covers everything you need. You may need to verify this with the vendor or instructor.

- For the curriculum you teach directly, review the teacher's manual to see if there is a recommended pace.

- Look for common themes and topics across subject areas and try to arrange them to be taught together if possible. For example, if earth science appears at the end of your science curriculum but your literature class covers a book about planets at the beginning of the year, explore ways to align them in the same time frame.

- Consider extracurricular activities like enrichment classes, sports, family trips, and planned important moments as opportunities to emphasize learning topics. For example, Ramadan is a religious holiday that includes themes of the moon phases. This can be taught with earth sciences.

When creating a pacing guide, it's crucial to remain flexible as life events, unexpected challenges, and varying learning paces necessitate adjustments. If certain subjects cannot fit within the time frame, consider carrying them over to the following school year. You can also dedicate time during holiday breaks or shorten the assignments to focus only on areas that you believe are key. Remember, this is your school, so run at your pace.

* * *

MINIMUM FOCUSED LEARNING TIME

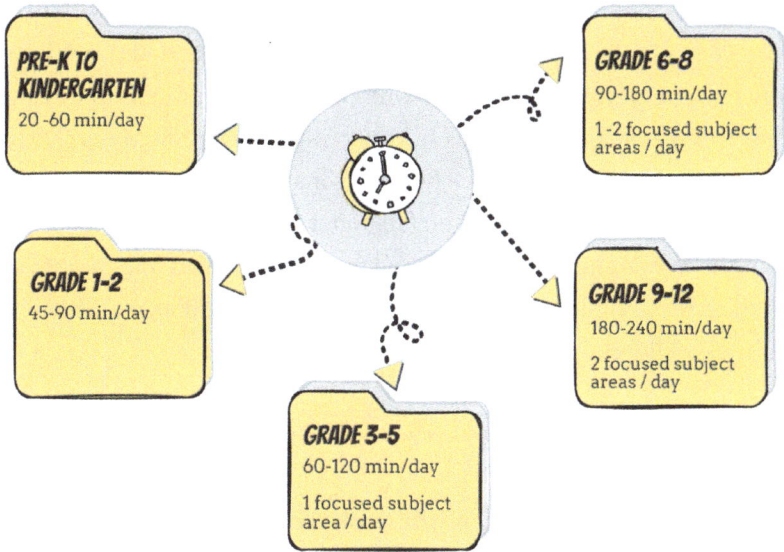

PRE-K TO KINDERGARTEN
20-60 min/day

GRADE 6-8
90-180 min/day

1-2 focused subject areas / day

GRADE 1-2
45-90 min/day

GRADE 9-12
180-240 min/day

2 focused subject areas / day

GRADE 3-5
60-120 min/day

1 focused subject area / day

* * *

Rhythm

Once you have your pacing guide, insert it into your calendar. There is no right answer and it's not expected that you will always stick to a pattern. The key is to be intentional and adjust early while maintaining a sense of predictability your child can follow. Here are some examples based on various working parent personas.

For The "Laptop Class"

The "laptop class" is a terminology that became popularized during the COVID-19 era, referring to people who can work remotely with little requirement to be onsite to complete their jobs. They include traditional office workers and entrepreneurs who can interact through laptops and smartphones without negatively impacting their productivity. Many have not returned to the office full-time, maintaining a fully remote or hybrid work model. Parents who fall under the laptop class will need to plan the homeschool schedule to make room for them to concentrate on their work while creating an equally effective learning environment for their children.

There are three main days to sequence for the laptop class:

1. ***Office Day*** - On this day, while you are in the office, your child is scheduled for in-person activities, including classes, co-ops, and subject-focused pods.
2. ***Home Day***—You continue your work commitments but block off certain parts of the day, offering 45 minutes—1 hour of side-by-side assistance with your child's assignment. In between, your child is doing independent work, taking online classes, or pursuing a personal passion (which may or may not be related to learning objectives).
3. ***Rest Day*** - Your child is engaged in something fun. It can overlap with an existing learning subject (because that's the best thing about homeschooling), but they are not expected to be "activated." In our house, those are Friday and Saturday, with Sunday being

the time I can focus on starting the week right with them. But in general, Rest Day is made for both of you to rest from your commitments to each other. They rest, and so do you.

MON-FRI WORKWEEK

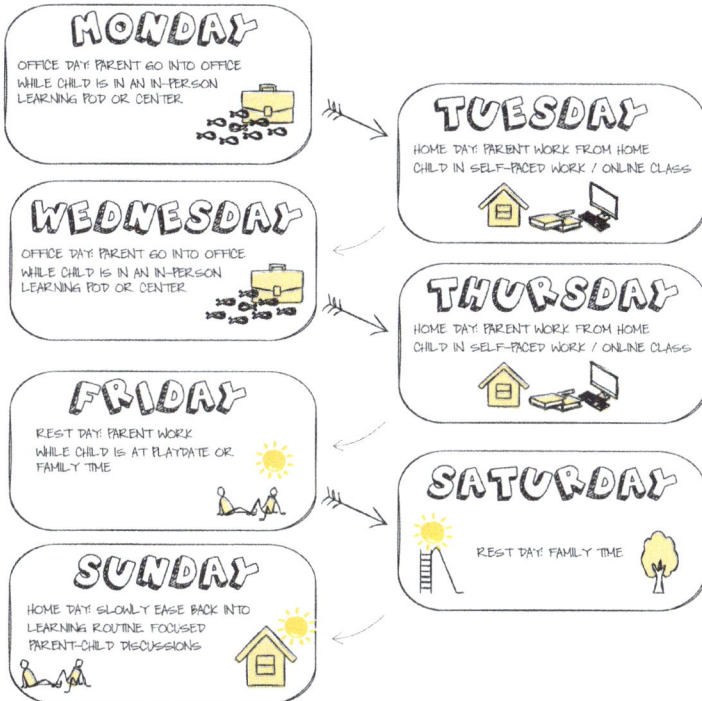

MONDAY
OFFICE DAY: PARENT GO INTO OFFICE WHILE CHILD IS IN AN IN-PERSON LEARNING POD OR CENTER

TUESDAY
HOME DAY: PARENT WORK FROM HOME CHILD IN SELF-PACED WORK / ONLINE CLASS

WEDNESDAY
OFFICE DAY: PARENT GO INTO OFFICE WHILE CHILD IS IN AN IN-PERSON LEARNING POD OR CENTER

THURSDAY
HOME DAY: PARENT WORK FROM HOME CHILD IN SELF-PACED WORK / ONLINE CLASS

FRIDAY
REST DAY: PARENT WORK WHILE CHILD IS AT PLAYDATE OR FAMILY TIME

SATURDAY
REST DAY: FAMILY TIME

SUNDAY
HOME DAY: SLOWLY EASE BACK INTO LEARNING ROUTINE. FOCUSED PARENT-CHILD DISCUSSIONS

How The Week Runs In My Home (Laptop Class)

Let's take a real example and allow me to share how my house ran in a typical week when my two daughters were in the 2nd and 5th grades:

Home Day

Mondays are usually full of meetings, and the workday will run long because I collaborate with teams in different time zones, requiring me to work late into the evenings. The good part is that while my husband needs to be in the office, I'll be working from home, and we both start our day at 6:00 am, with the expectation that kids will be up by 8:00 am. At that time, they are expected to check the agenda board in our living room to confirm the usual routine and get highlights of anything different that will happen that day. The normal instructions read, "Hygiene, morning chores, and get ready for breakfast." By 8:45 am, I will update my online status to "Away," giving myself a 15-minute break to greet the kids and conduct a breathing exercise to start the day.

Once our morning ceremony ends, I pivot back to work, and the girls will finish up their self-paced assignments. Today, it is online math problems and reading book chapters for language arts. They can take breaks but will only choose from the break activities options listed under the whiteboard. Right before lunch, each will attend an online session. Today, my 5th Grader has a tutoring session over a video conference call with Emily, the college student we met through our homeschool network who is mastering mathematics. My 2nd Grader logs into a virtual class where kids meet to build and share their Lego creations.

There are no leftovers from the night before, so I order lunch through an online food delivery. I make sure there's an order for Grandpa, who reaches the house just in time to join us for lunch. My calendar blocked 45 minutes for lunch, so I returned to my laptop. Meanwhile, the girls join their grandfather outside, where he is moving compost over to another part of the yard today, and the girls can go through an involved conversation about soil health and worms with him.

By 3:30 pm, Grandpa returns the children indoors while I wrap up my afternoon meeting. They're given a rest period, eat an afternoon snack, and play outside.

By 4:30 p.m., my husband returns home, and the kids have their gear ready for soccer practice. Everyone convenes at home by 6:30 p.m., washes up, has dinner, and winds down our day.

Office Day

Both parents need to be in their respective offices. After breakfast, the girls are taken by their father to their respective classes; our 2nd Grader to science class offered by the local animal rehabilitation center and our 5th Grader to language arts instructed by a warm piano teacher who is well known in the area for graduating homeschooled students through the renowned curriculum from the Institute of Excellence in Writing. Her house reserves a space that hosts up to 12 students per class, and families from as far as 30 miles away have enrolled for the year.

Both classes will end before noon, at which time my husband, given his proximity to the learning centers, can circle back to pick up the kids. Together, we can have lunch at the nearby fish and chips restaurant. Then, the girls are dropped off at a fellow homeschool family's house, whom we met from a learning pod with children of similar ages. There, they spend time in the large backyard, getting messy in the dirt and making believe.

By 4:00 pm, I pick them up on my way back from the office. We wash up and have dinner. Given it is World Refugee Day, I reserve that night's family bedtime reading to complete a beautiful graphic novel, When Victoria Jamieson and Omar Mohamed Scatter Stars, that chronicles the life of two Somalian orphans and their adventures in a refugee camp. Then, we reflect on our family history with commitments from each child to journal about what we have learned the following day. My 2nd Grader will turn in handwritten work that includes an illustration, and my 5th Grader can choose to turn in a one-pager or presentation that provides additional research she was able to find online.

"Do I tell my work I'm homeschooling?" This answer will vary depending on your company culture and employment status. My working hours vary as I manage relationships across various time zones. This allows me to build out my schedule if I can demonstrate productivity. While the conversation about what work should look like is growing, there are still no laws or protection (as of yet) for the working parent who wishes to homeschool.

Rest Day

Rest day reflects precisely what the children do. There are no expectations to do schoolwork, although learning continues in different forms. Rest day on Friday may mean the children will spend the first half of the day at an outdoor school focused on nature-based play with opportunities to interact with farm animals. When they return by 2:00 pm, I will have wrapped up my work early and expect to receive them both, along with four other homeschool friends who join us for Friday crepes. They'll help mix the batter and use their knowledge of measurement and heat to fry the perfect crepes. Everyone is expected to chip in by getting plates and cutting fruits to prepare the table.

The Home Day Before Work Week

With Fridays and Saturdays as full rest days, Sundays are purposed for focused project work and when my husband and I can prepare for the following week. On this day, the children are given space to catch up on assignments, complete problems requiring involved guidance from parents, or join in a special one-day course worth attending. It's worth noting that while we work to protect that day to be quiet to transition back to routine, we also ensure flexibility, as other weekend events can pop up as they often do on Sundays (birthday parties, scout meetings, gatherings with extended family).

The 4/10's

This refers to parents who work four 10-hour shifts in a week. Traditionally, they include nurses, government jobs, and factory and mechanic workers, with weekend hours. There are three types of days for this working parent persona:

1. *4/10 Day*—Since you will be completely unavailable, your child can benefit from enrolling in a co-op, micro-school, or learning pod. If your work schedule extends to Saturdays, consider onsite classes that offer enrichment activities. Math and language arts centers are open at these times, and personal tutors can also be arranged.
2. *Home Day*—While you are resting at home, block specific parts

of the day to offer 45-minute—1 hour of side-by-side assistance with your child's assignments. This is an opportunity to bond and concentrate discussions on key learning objectives.

3. **Rest Day** - It has been a long, full week, and both you and your child can unplug and decompress.

Those scheduled with 4/10s will likely have a short window for parent-instructed learning. Nevertheless, homeschooling can be accessible with options such as including micro-schools or pods within the week. In addition, you can arrange the learning period so that there are times of concentrated work and times that can be more relaxed and require less attention.

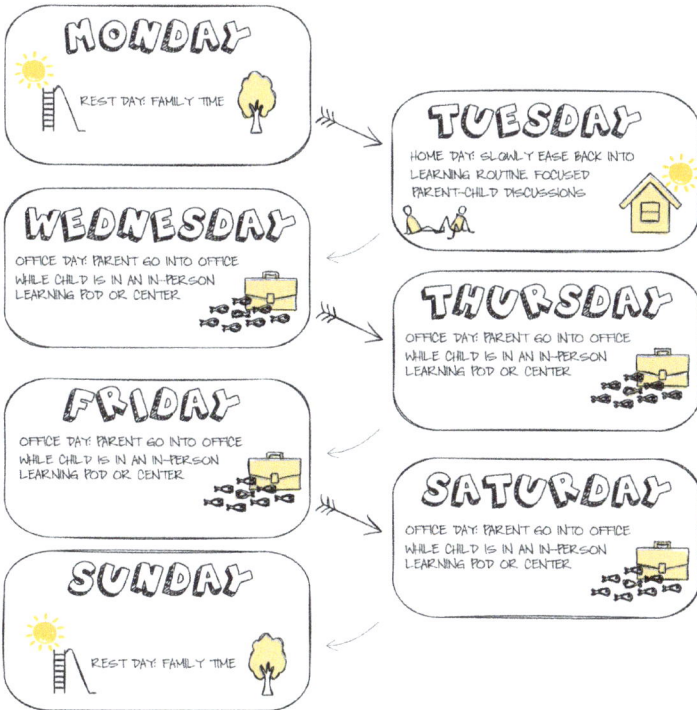

FOUR-10'S SCHEDULE

MONDAY — REST DAY. FAMILY TIME

TUESDAY — HOME DAY: SLOWLY EASE BACK INTO LEARNING ROUTINE. FOCUSED PARENT-CHILD DISCUSSIONS

WEDNESDAY — OFFICE DAY: PARENT GO INTO OFFICE WHILE CHILD IS IN AN IN-PERSON LEARNING POD OR CENTER

THURSDAY — OFFICE DAY: PARENT GO INTO OFFICE WHILE CHILD IS IN AN IN-PERSON LEARNING POD OR CENTER

FRIDAY — OFFICE DAY: PARENT GO INTO OFFICE WHILE CHILD IS IN AN IN-PERSON LEARNING POD OR CENTER

SATURDAY — OFFICE DAY: PARENT GO INTO OFFICE WHILE CHILD IS IN AN IN-PERSON LEARNING POD OR CENTER

SUNDAY — REST DAY. FAMILY TIME

For The Entrepreneur

For the sole proprietor, start-up CEO, or serial entrepreneur, you can dictate your schedules, making homeschooling while working very accessible. You can choose to be the parent instructor for all subjects or mix and match with learning pods, subject-specific classes, or tutors. While you have more flexibility, there is still a benefit in creating a predictable rhythm, blocking periods where your attention is to your learning child and periods reserved for business. In our house, my husband is a business owner and will incorporate teachings about how his business works and world economic news into lessons introducing financial literacy.

The options above share ideas on how working parents can organize their day with principles of achieving learning goals and predictability in mind. Depending on your work's expectations of you, your child's school week may not be the traditional Monday through Friday, and this is the beauty of homeschooling. Our weekends start on Thursday night in our home, and we spend Sunday mornings getting back into the school week. In all cases, you may be able to drop off your child to an on-site enrichment class or transfer that responsibility to a trusted adult.

Calendaring

Another way to approach time management is effectively using the calendar. Technology has catapulted the art of scheduling, and many calendar applications compete for your attention. Solutions like Microsoft CoPilot can suggest, based on the availability on your calendar, which times and days work best for specific events. Monday.com is a solution that helps you visualize how much time you and your child are spending on specific activities. I find Google Calendar quite helpful, and I leverage its labeling, color coding, and calendar-sharing features daily to organize my and my children's days. As they've gotten older, they are now taking control of updating their schedules, which I can view and adjust.

When planning for a specific day, I want to ensure my children follow a daily "inhale-exhale" rhythm. Inhale activities are cerebral and usually occur inside, while exhale activities use body movement and are usually located in nature. Examples of inhale activities include focused schoolwork, zoom classes, reading, writing, and discussions on topics. Examples of exhaling activities could be exploring the outdoors, playing in the playground, recess, nature classes, going to the theater, playing musical instruments, and doing sports.

With this mindset and a well-structured calendar, I can easily tell whether my children receive a balanced day. For example, if we're not having a sports day, I'll make sure to include an outing or a lab outside of the house. This breaks up the sense of confinement a child can experience if they are inside for too long.

In summary, maximize the features of your online calendar, including juxtaposing multiple calendars into one view, using color coding to distinguish activity types, implementing naming conventions for your meeting titles so they're easily searchable, and tracking your progress through tasks. You will start to see patterns that may prompt you to adjust and, most importantly, make room to rest.

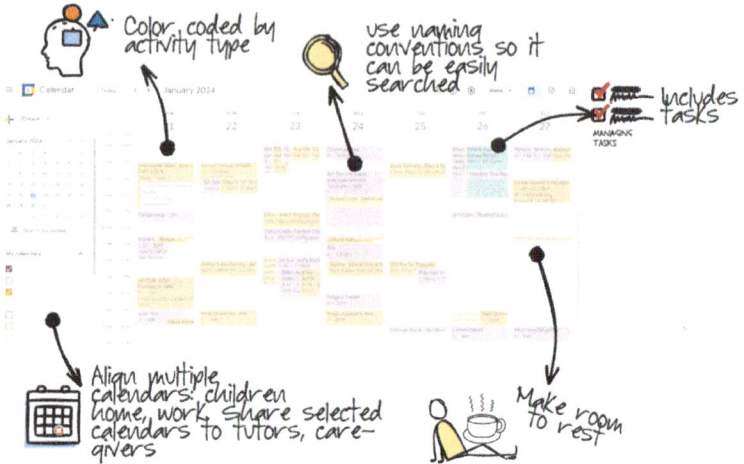

SELECTED CALENDAR FEATURES

Color coded by activity type

use naming conventions, so it can be easily searched

Includes tasks

MANAGING TASKS

Align multiple calendars: children home, work. Share selected calendars to tutors, care-givers

Make room to rest

Delegating

Let's not do this alone. Having a career and driving the educational experience for your child can be overwhelming without the help of others. Similar to the working world, outsourcing is used to delegate your responsibilities so you can maximize your time towards what is most important while keeping things manageable and sustainable.

Balance. Stress will impact your effectiveness in carrying both the homeschool commitments you have with your child and the work commitments you have for yourself. By delegating responsibilities so that you only engage in moments that matter, you can eliminate tension, allowing space for the positive environment necessary to carry out this incredible journey with your child. Additionally, the sense of balance you gain from delegation will contribute to you and your child's well-being.

Cost-effective. Delegating can sound costly when you consider paying for services. Still, the benefits can address your concerns if you analyze and re-purpose your existing budget to tailor it to your "homeschool while working" lifestyle. For parents who budgeted for private school, extracurricular activities, and caregiving, you'll be surprised to find savings available when you're no longer paying for private school tuition, and you can expand on your caregiver's role to support your child through the new school agenda. With your homeschool network, you can also exercise the power of collective bargaining to negotiate class prices to a discounted level. This mainly works with micro-schools and with vendors who are sole proprietors.

Sustainable. Homeschooling is a commitment to at least one school year. That can be from ten months to an entire fiscal year. This means delegating a portion of your responsibilities should be a serious consideration. Can you outsource some of the administrative activities around your home? Can you rely on the services or networks around you to support you year-round? Think about the help you will need in the long term.

Delegation can happen in many forms. Below are a few ways to consider.

Lean On Family

This is the first site of support if you have trusted family members who can commit to the portion of your schedule that you need help with. Grandparents, aunts, uncles, and even older siblings can help drop off your child to a one-hour learning pod or assist them with assignments. Additionally, simply having family members around will add to the learning experience. In my home, Grandpa loves to come over and paint in his free time, and the children naturally gravitate to his presence, where they converse about color and art history.

Connect With Community

Community members are an extension of your family and can be trusted similarly. The most efficient way is to pair your child with families who also homeschool. This can create a divide-and-conquer system with fellow parents, where you each take turns teaching or driving the children to their learning sessions (i.e., co-ops). It also creates a natural study group, even if they are focusing on different topics.

When you and your child have access to a strong community, it plays a pivotal role in providing support, fostering socialization, and enriching educational experiences. That's why a key part of a successful homeschool journey is to have strong, authentic connections with a homeschooling community. Through this, you foster a fantastic environment with people you trust and where your child can grow up safely in a nurturing environment.

In addition to opportunities to socialize, share learning materials, and coordinate class enrollments, community connections also open doors to specialized learning opportunities that may otherwise be challenging to access. Through my own experiences and observing events posted in social media groups, I am floored by the types of activities curated by motivated homeschool communities. People organize workshops, guest speakers, and classes taught by experts in various fields. This past spring, a group of parents from our learning pod convinced the nearby museum to host children from 3rd to 7th grade to learn about the California Gold Rush. This included a dedicated speaker and workshop on brick-making and prospecting for gold to mimic the early settlers.

It can be difficult for some of us to access this environment, especially in larger cities where people are transient, and relationships are more widely spread. However, with a continued increase in homeschooling families, building connections initiated through social media is getting easier. I've met many amazing working parents who live nearby through Facebook and WhatsApp groups. These relationships usually entail a rendezvous at a joint homeschool event and, later, planned parent-child playdates where we can learn about each other. Not all meetups will lead to lasting friendships, but I always gain deeper insights into how different families navigate the homeschool world. And for the playdates that develop into more, these relationships can last for many years with individuals who collaborate and help each other create the best experiences for their children.

Enroll Your Child In Classes

While some may argue that enrolling your child in classes is not considered homeschooling, I say it is. Parents still have control of the child's overall curriculum for the year, selecting what and who is teaching specific subjects. These services will give you several hours to focus on work, whether online or in person. Many homeschool pods and micro-schools will host classes for several hours a day. This, paired with scheduled play dates, homework groups, and enrichment activities, will open up dedicated working hours for you.

Expand The Role Of Your Caregiver

Nannies, babysitters, and au pairs can also be trained to assist with your homeschool routine. You may need to re-calibrate your search to make sure the hires have the right skills. For the most part, general skills to look for are effective communication, patience, creativity, and willingness to collaborate with parents to ensure the education routine is consistent and effective. This will be sufficient for children in Grade 2 and under. For children in grades 3 to 5, I recommend hiring someone who can go through instructions with your child. This way, you can allocate times when your child can work independently without oversight. For middle and high school students, having someone knowledgeable in one or more subject areas can provide your child with additional support at home to work through projects or tackle challenging problems.

I have gone through several caregivers and changed my requirements when we adopted the homeschool model. Instead of someone who can babysit and do house chores, I adjusted my search to find a "Homeschool Family Assistant." These are candidates currently enrolled in college and willing to work part-time, specifically at the beginning of the day. I find college students are already in the academic mindset and come with a certain level of computer skills and, with minimal training, will know how to use online calendars, documents, and spreadsheets to help me track my children's progress and adjust their curricula. To assist with dropping off the kids at their local activities and classes, your assistant must have a safe driving record and be comfortable guiding them through their school assignments. Because this person is in college, I expect they will remember and be able to answer questions for subjects under the Grade 6 level. Unless this person masters math or science, I will pair my children with specialized tutors for these subjects instead of relying on the Family Assistant alone. Below is a sample checklist for a Homeschool Family Assistant for children up to Grade 7. As my children are growing older, my requirements for the Family Assistant evolve to align with their needs.

HOMESCHOOL FAMILY ASSISTANT

In search for an authentic, talented, multi-tasking Family Assistant for our homeschool family

What We Need

- ✓ Familiar with online calendars & and spreadsheets
- ✓ Great driving record to usher kids to activities
- ✓ Comfortable tutoring elementary school age children
- ✓ Bonus: Knows another language or plays musical instrument

Ideal candidate

Currently pursuing higher education/in college or has experience with tutoring/education

Outsource House Responsibilities

The gig economy, known for short-term contracts and freelance work, has evolved to truly benefit the work-from-home persona, especially for homeschool parents. Whether it's services for installing furniture, grocery shopping, delivering dinner, or washing your laundry, you can outsource a good portion of your household responsibilities to make room for parent-child learning moments. Consider using these services, so you have more time to focus on both your professional and homeschool responsibilities.

In summary, effective time management requires being oriented to the resources available and having the know-how to use them effectively. It will take some time upfront, but when done well, it will pay off.

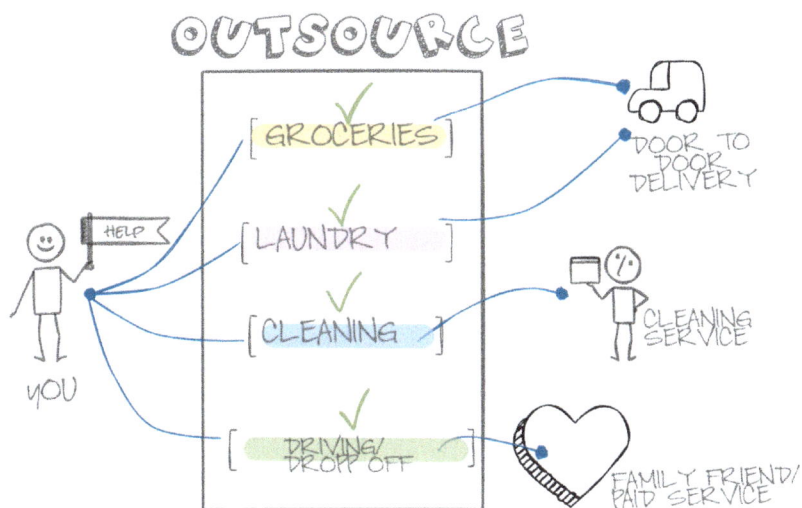

8

How Much Will This Cost Me?

A recent study published in 2021 by Lending Tree revealed that raising a child costs an average of $21,681, and families should expect to spend over $230,000 before that child turns 18. This calculation covered many categories but did not explicitly state what portion of the costs is for education-related spending, which makes me assume that the cost is likely higher.

For homeschooling, Tutors.com reports this can range between $600 to $70,000 per child per annum, illustrating there is a broad scope in how homeschooling can be delivered. A family can choose to spend as little as possible, with a parent committing full-time to delivering their child's education, or on the other end, they can outsource all responsibilities by hiring a private tutor dedicated to sourcing premium material and expensive extra-curricular activities. What you choose depends on your own lifestyle, what your homeschooling objectives are, and what resources are available to you.

You can redirect portions of your child's education budget towards homeschool needs without adding any more to your overall spending.

This especially works for parents who have committed savings towards private school, after-school activities, and child care. In our case, we originally planned for tuition costs for two children through high school. In addition, we expected costs for field trips and extra-curricular activities. After we decided to homeschool, we managed to repurpose our school tuition budget towards a part-time homeschool family assistant, supplies, and select classes planned for certain times of the year. We managed to hold onto much of our savings as our state-funded charter homeschool offered a stipend worth $2,700 for curriculum and supplies. We built relationships with homeschool families who partnered with us to coordinate play dates and gatherings that could easily resemble ad hoc childcare - for free!

Effectively, we reduced our spending to 70% of our original budget, enjoying flexibility in increasing and decreasing our costs throughout the school year without compromising the quality of our children's education.

Find Free Things

Whether it's the curriculum, manipulative, books, or even school furniture, you can find practically anything for free these days. Neighborhood apps, social media, or even posted signs you can find at coffee shops will offer anything from books, manipulatives, supplemental equipment, and even furniture. Homeschool communities tend to offer the materials they use at the beginning or the end of the school year as they clean out their space in preparation for their child's next grade. I particularly enjoy attending book-return fairs hosted by homeschool families. Here, people get to meet in person to pick up or drop off their used books and get advice on how to use the materials best.

Available Online

Online classes can be free and paid. TeachersPayTeachers and Khan Academy are excellent portals that offer both these options. Your local library and non-profit organizations like the National Aeronautics and Space Administration (NASA) house fantastic learning modules. I've also seen homegrown approaches where parents record Zoom instructions for their first child, which are later passed on as online material for the younger sibling. In my experience, I find free online tools great as supplemental to my curriculum.

Paid online material can also be more cost-effective than in-person classes. Some vendors offering both will offer virtual classes at a discounted rate, but there are trade-offs. For example, learning and social circles that occur entirely in virtual settings are more engineered, whereas learning through osmosis and friendship may occur more naturally in in-person settings. Online content is also helpful when traveling. Whether you have a self-paced curriculum or virtual calls with an instructor, you can adjust schedules to meet your needs.

Share costs

Co-ops, micro-schools, and communities last because families benefit from sharing costs for keeping these gatherings going. As a collective, we have strong purchasing power and negotiation positions to source amazing classes for our children. I was fortunate to be part of a strong parent group that influenced the nearby botanical establishment to host a six-week course on plant science. Later that spring, another parent group inspired the local museum to curate a full-day workshop dedicated to learning about the California Gold Rush. While my 4th Grader learned how to make bricks and sift for fools' gold, I spent my day in the office at a team meeting.

Another way to share costs is to rotate used materials around families. The best part about homeschool circles is that we default to sharing knowledge and resources. It's ideal when families have children across several age groups, and opportunities to learn from each other, borrow, and hand down used items are frequent.

Negotiate With Instructors

The supply of educators can come through many networks you come in contact with. You and fellow homeschool parents can negotiate rates with vendors, tutors, and even PhD students with your prescriptive approach or request that they come up with the specific syllabus to teach.

One family living near a well-known college source most of her curriculum from PhD students who curate syllabi tailored for their children. Throughout the week, their house rotates through Masters and PhD students who come in person to teach their lessons. The overall costs of these in-person tutor experiences can vary, and, depending on your negotiating skills, this route can cost less than traditional vendors.

Avoid Peak Prices

The first savings we realized when we began to homeschool was our ability to avoid high prices charged by education and aftercare services during peak times of the day. For example, gym access for certain sports will open at 2:00 pm but will expect most people to come in after 4:00 pm. Consider signing up for classes in the earlier parts of the day. Visiting museums mid-week, driving up to the ski slopes outside school holidays, and traveling in low seasons will save your wallet and sanity as you avoid crowds.

Enroll With Charter Homeschools Schools Offering Funds

While this may not be true for all charter homeschools, we were fortunate to enroll in one that offered an annual stipend for curriculum and supplies. Typically, the funds will meet minimum needs, and you may only spend them on classes that are considered approved vendors by the school. However, consider it free money and the approved vendors tend to offer discounted prices for those using charter homeschool vouchers.

Prioritize What You Are Willing To Pay Premium For And When

Know that you can mix or phase in and out any of these options. Also, know that you are not confined to teaching every subject in the same learning period. For example, I will ensure that Language Arts and Math are covered weekly in the primary grades. However, with science, I will enroll for a paid course in the spring while offering general self-paced work, which only costs me the book. For exploration and sports, it will be a mix of community offerings that are usually very discounted and paid courses sprinkled throughout the year. This approach allows me to plan a full year's budget for only certain classes while spreading the costs to the others.

There will also be times when it is necessary to spend more time on one subject than another. When my daughter was having a hard time with algebra and it was clear she would not learn this subject well from me, we opted to increase the number of tutoring sessions for a period of time. Once my daughter demonstrated a sense of confidence, we reverted back to our regular schedule and spending.

People can homeschool at close to virtually no cost. But for a working parent, you'll likely need to budget for parts of it. The key is to know what you can pay for, what you can share, and what you're willing to do yourself.

9

Building Transcript For Higher Education

Homeschool students often pursue higher education after completing high school. The conversation about future academic paths typically begins between Grades 7 and 8, where families discuss potential college plans and extracurricular activities that set them apart. While it's essential not to pressure your child too early regarding college, developing "transcript scenarios" for one or two likely paths your child might take is beneficial.

Transcript scenarios involve mapping out college requirements for the courses, activities, and test scores your child plans to complete before graduating. Colleges generally look for advanced coursework, extracurricular programs, strong test scores, letters of recommendation, and personal essays. This planning process is best done with the guidance of an expert in college admissions, such as a high school counselor, or procure college counseling services, such as InGenius Prep or Zenith Prep. State-funded homeschool programs often provide access to admissions counselors, and independent homeschoolers can seek consultation through private services.

A key advantage of homeschooling is that it gives students the unique opportunity to pursue interests early without having to accommodate the traditional school schedules. Your child can immerse in diverse learning opportunities, such as arts, sports, internships, volunteer work, and civic engagement, that showcase their well-roundness.

For students who discover their passion and talent early, parents can adjust their homeschool schedule to their needs. I recall a friend whose sons were talented swimmers, and it was clear winning in the waters would be their entry ticket to college. Both working parents established a school schedule sandwiched by swim classes to support their swimming career. Fast forward seven years later, their transcript included advanced placement classes, swim awards, and summer jobs at the community pool.

In another example, a friend moved their daughter to an online high school after eight years of in-person homeschooling. This gave her daughter room to pursue her passion for playing with the city symphony and qualified her to apply for a well-known music college.

To create a compelling transcript, meticulously document your child's achievements, awards, and test scores. This comprehensive record will help build a strong case for their readiness for college and support a narrative of how they plan to contribute to society. No matter the path taken, you will have provided an exceptional homeschool experience, preparing confident, well-rounded young adults ready to make positive contributions to the world.

10

Conclusion

When I share with parents that there is a way to homeschool and work, many initially think it's a lot of work. While it can initially appear complicated, it's not complex. Using your existing time management, planning, and organization skills, you can craft a personalized educational journey that caters to your child's needs and passions. I also hope you can see that by taking advantage of technology, community, and existing services, you can outsource parts in such a way as to accommodate your work schedule.

In this book, I introduce you to different approaches, tools, and real-world scenarios that showcase how you can effectively homeschool while still excelling in your career. From grasping state guidelines and establishing a robust support system to incorporating technology and delegating certain educational tasks, I hope that through each chapter, you've begun to visualize the possibilities of homeschooling while you work.

As you progress, may you discover joy in small achievements, strength during tough times, and satisfaction in knowing that you are making a meaningful impact on your child's life. Cheers to a voyage filled with learning opportunities, personal growth, and infinite possibilities. Sending you best wishes on your homeschooling endeavor; may it strengthen the bonds within your family and cultivate a lifelong passion for learning and exploration.

You've got this!!

References

AbilityPath. (n.d.). *Children's learning styles.* https://abilitypath.org/ap-resources/childrens-learning-styles/

Cattanach, J. (2023, September 11). *Annual costs to raise a small child increased by 19.3% nationwide to $21,681 between 2016 and 2021.* Lending Tree. https://www.lendingtree.com/debt-consolidation/raising-a-child-study/

DeGuerin, Mack (2019, July 17). *17 famous people who were home-schooled.* Business Insider. https://www.businessinsider.com/17-famous-people-who-were-home-schooled-2019-7

Gilchrist, K. (2018, July 19). *Advice for entrepreneurs: Habits from homeschool CEO Richard Lorenzen.* CNBC. https://www.cnbc.com/2018/07/19/advice-for-entrepreneurs-habits-from-homeschool-ceo-richard-lorenzen.html

Famous Homeschoolers. (n.d.). *Business Entrepreneurs.* http://www.famoushomeschoolers.net/entrepreneurs.html

Murez, C. (2024, January 16). *1 in 5 U.S. parents worry their teen is addicted to the internet.* US News. https://www.usnews.com/news/health-news/articles/2023-10-30/1-in-5-u-s-parents-worry-their-teen-is-addicted-to-the-internet

Ray, B. D.. (2024, May 29). *Research facts on homeschooling, homeschool fast facts.* National Home Education Research Institute. https://www.nheri.org/research-facts-on-homeschooling/

Smith, A. G., Campbell, J. (2023, May 31). *Homeschooling is on the rise, even as the pandemic recedes.* Reason Foundation. https://reason.org/commentary/homeschooling-is-on-the-rise-even-as-the-pandemic-recedes/

Soifer, D. (2022, December 28). *The "get to know 5" bold microschool predictions for 2023.* National Microschooling Center. https://microschoolingcenter.org/news-blog/predictions

Watson, Andrew. (2023, September 17) *Getting the principles just right: classroom decoration.* Learning and the Brain. https://www.learningandthebrain.com/blog/getting-the-principles-just-right-classroom-decoration/

Weimar, Lynn. (2023, January 12). *I homeschooled my son, now a successful businessman: Nathan Barry.* Newsweek. https://www.newsweek.com/i-homeschooled-my-son-now-successful-businessman-nathan-barry-1777180

Hazen, Tamatha. (2023, May 24). *Average Cost of Homeschooling.* Tutors.com https://tutors.com/costs/homeschooling-cost

Curriculum Example

The following illustration is a curriculum map of two core subjects for my fifth grader. Note you may want to include specific exploratory subjects like music, theater, language or sports if you have specific objectives for those areas. A few items to point out:

Learning Period: The learning period can be of any unit (monthly, weekly, quarterly). I recommend nothing smaller than two weeks to a month to allow for flexibility for unplanned events that requires you to adjust.

In-Person Class: For in-person classes, obtain the instructor syllabus and map the assignments to the specific learning objective. The instructor will likely have the learning objective also mapped out which you can leverage.

Multiple Curricula: In the example below for Science, there are two curricula being used. Studies Weekly, in this example, is planned to be parent-instructed. It is supplemented by an online Outschool class call "Intro to Chemistry".

Diagnostics: Different from "tests" and "exams", time is reserved to assess the child's using a professional assessment solution. This can be done in-person or online, depending on the vendor you select.

SAMPLE CURRICULUM MAP

SUBJECT	CURRICULA	LEARNING PERIOD 1	LEARNING PERIOD 2
LANGUAGE ARTS ①	*INSTITUTE OF EXCELLENCE IN WRITING ANCIENTS GRADE 5*	*Classic myths pages 9-72* *Ancients Checklist Lesson 1-21* *Diagramming Sentences A* *Greek & Latin Roots 1-20*	*Ancients Lesson 22-40* *Lesson 9: The Epic of Gilgamesh* *Diagramming Sentences B* *Greek & Latin Roots 21-40*
	FOCUSED STANDARD	*RCWA: Phonics* *LACA: Language Conv.*	*RCKA: Key Ideas* *WONA: Writing Opinion*
② **SCIENCE**	*STUDIES WEEKLY SCIENCE GRADE 5*	*Structures & Properties of Matter*	*Matter & Energy in Organisms & Ecosystems*
	OUTSCHOOL: INTRO TO CHEMISTRY	*Introduction to the Periodic Table*	*Naming Chemical Compounds*
③	*FOCUSED STANDARD*	*MAIB: Matter & Interaction B* *ENYA: Energy A*	*ECOA: Ecosystems A*
DIAGNOSTICS	*IXL DIAGNOSTICS*		*DIAGNOSTIC #1*

① In-person class   ② Mix of online & parent instructed   ③ Learning objective

About the Author

Together with her husband, FH Inanlou homeschools her two daughters in the Bay Area of California while successfully pursuing a corporate career and managing a portfolio of family businesses. She is an experienced project manager and certified in process improvement methodologies, which she uses to help corporations and non-profit organizations solve efficiency problems. She is fully aware of the superpowers that exist in all of us, especially parents who work and homeschool their children. She has helped countless working parents re-look at their resources and the same 24 hours we are all given to fully make the most out of their homeschool day without compromising their professional pursuits.

You can connect with me on:
🌐 https://www.homeschoolandworking.com

Made in the USA
Las Vegas, NV
05 February 2025